THE MYTH OF CURIOSITY.

'THE ODE TO IMAGINATION! '

ARNAV RAJSINGH

Copyright © Arnav Rajsingh
All Rights Reserved.

To My Parents, Teachers and Classmates who inspired me to write this book.

"You're off to great places, today is your day. Your mountain is waiting, so get on your way.

<u>*Dr. Seuss: Author/Poet*</u>*"*

Contents

Foreword

Preface

One day, after doing my Mathematics homework. I found a diary lying around my table. I had to write a limmeric as English homework.So, I took my pencil and tried to think a lot about it. I wrote something that my parent called my first creation. They then got me many books about different poeple. This got me immersed into reading books. I read through different generes, romance, sci-fi, experimental, fictional comedy and biographies.I felt like going into a crazy world where anything could happen and all my thoughts flew away. This got me writing poems and after that it felt as if words would flow out of my pencil and on the paper. I selected some poems to be featured in this book. I love reading books and now I'm writing one.Ha,how the time changes.

Arnav Raj Singh

Acknowledgements

To My Parents who supported me.

   To My English Teachers who encourage me.

   To My Classmates who gave me ideas.

   And you reader who help me to reach out to others.

   Thanks a lot to you all.

   "Never regret anything that made you smile"

1. A Moonless Night

It was a hard night as the moon was on sleep
and Earth was waiting for a light
While the nightwalkers arose
The wolf crept underneath to jump on the prey
In Acacia wood of Ol' Klatay
As the bats snapped their wings
and owls hooted near the springs
As Sherlock searches for footsteps
the Monkey crack Dad Jokes
The Lion wants a chance to kill all the antelopes
While Steve and Alex sleep in tents
and Brittany finds trashy vents
But the mystery remains
There's a monster in the drain
No one knows who he is
No one knows why he is

2. Inside The Heart

Deep down within, where the core resides
live the souls trapped
Those bodyless creatures
Roaming around to be used again
With thy face gloomy
Waiting for thy savior
Work, all days and nights
for the one above
Never do they rest
Pride on their faces
While people come and go
the soul lives billions
The mindless creatures
Fiddling with themselves
Never do they look behind
the're one of those kinds
Jumping from one body to another

3. Dumpster Party

When the Sun drifts away
and Moon shines bright as anything
The Racoons heist on the dumpster
like a masked scavenger
They eat and party like brats
Then they paw cute pet cats
The Next shifts are Fox
sly as they can be,quieter than a mouse
Poking 'round, they escape traps
sometimes the Racoons join in
dancing all over the garbage bin
When they get bored and sleepy
Tiny Squeaks come out
and then they picnic and rome around
all big enough to give us jump scares
Then at last
Smallest than all
bugging out from the wall
the insects who eat everything up
Rumour is, they burp!
Sometimes they become snacks for frogs
Stupid as they are

THE MYTH OF CURIOSITY.

Those goofy water hogs
always soggy and wet
But during the day they all keep away
They meet on Tuesdays
and slug around the way
and swim in garbage
In May

4. The House of My Dreams

Besides the noisy brook
A hill so full of water
As the tremendous house lies within
In a tiny hut where one god must've lived
The bright light ahead
As Sun sends warm greetings
Where the beauty and beast live together
The house of your destiny
Where stars shine at the people with hope
and wars stay away
A place for a new journey
and happiness and harmony
Where age is just a number
all those who had the luck to live in this heaven
a priceless treasure
and a graceful pleasure
*Incredible creation of *Hephaestus*
Hephaestus is Greece of Fire and Invention

5. Earth

A Godly marvel
our home that thrives within
where our souls reside
A home to happiness
As love praises its beauty
As the shine of Dawn glimmers through
Which gives each a home a personality
Where we meet our inner self
our start, our end
A place to depend
The creation of thy God
His gift to nature
A place so the fascination
As the water paddles its way through
with twists and turns
there's a lot to learn
In the love of Mother Earth

6. A windy night

My First Poem

That night it was windy,
I was awake all the night
To my surprise, I saw someone sneaking
At first, I was a little scared
I did not even dare get out of Bed
Then I collected my courage
Oops! I was stuck to the old Bed
I then took a torch and got out of Bed
To the stairs I went slowly
Creak, Creak, Creak went the floors
Hush, went the wind
Squeak went a rat
I went to the kitchen to find out who it was
I thought I'd get a theif
I walked into mischief
It was my cheeky brother eating a choclate
I was a little angry

THE MYTH OF CURIOSITY.

I was scared for nothing?
Giving him a scolding I went back to sleep

• 8 •

7. I hear a beap

As I walked on the street

I hear a couple of beeps

But It wasn't me

I looked around but there was no one to see

Just Me and my doggy

I think the pranksters were at sea

I walked back home

Like Sherlock Holmes

No clue here

No clue there

What is this mystery

The weirdest prank in history

Soon we'll find out who is up to this

I slept soundly

but woke up spellbound

I could see my alarm having a fit of beeps

Why can't that annoying me thing let me have some good night's

sleep

8. My wonderful bag

I had a bag
Older than the oldest hag
Even though it was fantastic
And looked more realistic
Wanna know what was in it?
An old stick belonging to my dad
He was always grumpy and sad
An umbrella sat near the stick
It was very bright
Much to my delight
As intimidating as the rainbow
Thought the stick was only yellow
Also some bead made of leaves
As hard as a coconut
I used it to treat the guests who visited my hut
Then slept cool sunglass
As green as grass
Just to make me look cool
Back when I was in school
This was all in my bag

Older than the oldest hag

9. Mouse in the house

There is a troubling mouse
the terror of my house
It is probably a Rat
There is no one to chase her
Not even a Cat
That squeaky pest
makes a horrible mess
Mouse here, Mouse there
People, Beware!
Making a nest in rice
can't she just be nice
Oh Yeah! Do you think that is fun?
She troubles everyone
One day she gnawed at our bat
It was time to bring a Cat
A Cat was brought
Phew! The troublemaker was caught
I think she was a rodent fraud

10. Weeping for the trees

It was midnight

as I turned almost blind

I crept out of my house

I thought it was a bratty mouse

But to my suprise the trees were all gone

Just there was a sap weeping

The cause was humans

What a devastating scene it was

As it wept for forest gods

"There were many of our kind",he said

"Now it's just me and the flower bed"

11. Who is behind me?

It was 3 night
when I woke up suddenly
As I had forgotten to read a passage
and write the author a message
I switched on the light
and had a cup of tea
and felt as if someone was following me
Who wanted to follow me?
At the time three
Orges?Ghouls?Witches?
Buttersnuffles from the sea?
The thought itself made me yell
but no voice came
I was alone and had no one to tell
I felt as if Harry Potter casted a stunning spell
I took the shield of the brave and a stick Father found in a cave
I saw behind me, that there was nothing at all
It was my shadow, getting tall
What a fool I'm
It scared me like a rat small

12. Kite Runner

If I was a kite runner,
And have my passion
I would fly a kite that would swirl so high,
That birds won't see it fly
Witty I'll be with my kite,
That air and wind would have a fight
My kite would go breezing through,
That would make them look in awe like a pig
The aeroplane would be like a turtle to it for a bit,
It would be a rabbit
That is what I think when I sit,
That is what I want for a bit
Not ever gets stuck in the tree,
And it flies freely
Faster than wind it would be,
Flying above anything you see
Mount Everest would watch in awe,
News reporters would cry in awe
This record of mine would be in the record book,
And awesome to look

THE MYTH OF CURIOSITY.

For months it'll be on earth,
Then far away it would be
I'll fly because of it,
To planets you never see
My kite would be famous with me,
Even in the worlds of god you see
And swirl like anything,
Not even birds could do a thing and watch
And then every kiddie you see,
Would be playing games about me
That is what I dream of when I sit,
That is what I dream for a bit

13. Rainbow Valley

A world so full and happy
As the Redwoods stand by protecting
As Deers trample the muddy castle
The daisies all twiddle with wind
As the shallow rivers flow gently
The rainbows stretch abroad
All day and night with love in sight
The star of all the valleys
As trees cover the imperial grounds
For this is my Rainbow valley

14. Ice Cream Seller

Once in a poor family, lived a boy named Shyam. His father Ramnath, an ice-cream seller, sold his item just behind Shyam's school. His mother had died, so Ramnath married another woman who was cruel to shyam. In the school where shyam read, the teacher ate up all the lunch when the kids went to play. His stepmother gave him very less food and it was also eaten by the teacher. Ramnath's condition also became poor and thus his last days approached nearer and nearer. Shyam had to leave the school. He started to sell the ice-cream. The old grumby teacher thought that Shyam was a child, so he could fool Shyam. Shyam knew it so he made the van freezing cold. While Shyam was sleeping, the teacher kept his hand in the van and it froze. In the morning he found out this and complained the principal who fired out the teacher and gave his father medical check-up.

15. Those Tweeters

It was a evening of beauty,
That took away my heart
I could do nothing ,
But smile for a while
No problems to fear,
As I watched a group of Dear
All alone I was,
A mesmerising sight to see,
I heard Birds tweeting,
It was so lovely
I wondered and pondered if i could do the same,
But I didn't know it would be a hard game
A miracle of Nature, the magic of God
I plucked flowers and took a sniff,
As the lovers sing a melody
As the Cricket chirp,
The birds flew to my heart
What a beauty they are,
They sing like a Star

Sneak "pic" Of Ares 2059

ARES 2059
BY ARNAV RAJ SINGH

• 23 •